South Dakota

simply beautiful

Photography by J. C. Leacock

FARCOUNTRY
PRESS

ISBN: 1-56037-266-4

© 2003 Farcountry Press

Photography © by J. C. Leacock unless otherwise indicated.

For more information on our books write: Farcountry Press,
P.O. Box 5630, Helena, Montana 59604; call (800) 821-3874;
or visit www.farcountrypress.com.

Created, produced, and designed in the United States.
Printed in Korea.

FRONT COVER:
Clusters of purple dame's rockets decorate this hillside in Wind Cave National Park.

TITLE PAGE:
Quarterhorse mares and their foals share grazing space at Krogman Ranch in Mellette County.

ABOVE:
Badlands National Park protects 244,000 acres of these unique wind- and water-sculpted landforms.

FACING PAGE:
Some of the fastest animals in the world, pronghorns roam South Dakota's open prairies; when startled, these graceful animals can run up to 60 miles per hour.
PHOTO BY SOUTH DAKOTA TOURISM

Foreword

By J. C. Leacock

As a nature photographer, I've been to some of the most dramatically beautiful places in this country, from soaring peaks to rugged coastlines to red rock canyons. Yet one of the most beautiful nights I've ever enjoyed was spent camped next to a prairie pothole in Samuel H. Ordway, Jr. Memorial Preserve near Leola, South Dakota. The glowing fireflies, bird life, and the poetic juxtaposition of high prairie grass and water provided me with a lightshow scored by magical birdsongs that conveyed a natural harmony I shall never forget. You don't really expect to have these kinds of experiences in South Dakota, but if you open your eyes and mind, you shall experience it in all of its natural and cultural beauty.

South Dakota is a state of stunning diversity. The western part of the state truly is haunted by the echoes of the Old West. In less than a day's drive you can go from the mountainous beauty, western romance, and history of the Black Hills, Mt. Rushmore, Crazy Horse Mountain, and Deadwood to colorful and mysterious Badlands National Park. In the eastern part of the state, rolling farms and ranches give way to the more midwestern and relatively flatter farmland east of the mighty Missouri River. Here, whether it be a tractor museum, an old church, a classic red barn, or a prairie pothole rich with wildlife, beauty of remarkable variety can be found.

Another aspect of South Dakota that I love is the feeling that you are truly in the heartland of America. All of the good things that make America what it is—honesty, integrity, a work ethic, common sense, self-sufficiency, community, kindness—embody the essence of South Dakota. From a hometown rodeo in Wessington Springs to Billy's Café (best hash browns I've ever had) in Sisseton, people will treat you like you live next door. You find yourself in the heart of real America, and it feels good.

South Dakota has treated me well. It is my sincerest hope that through the images in this book, South Dakotans can feel a sense of pride for their state and visitors can not only use it as a guide for their travels, but take it with them in fond remembrance.

LEFT: South Dakota has trails for all levels of bicyclists: dirt paths up mountain slopes, single-tracks through rolling prairies, paved rails-to-trails, and twisting tracks through badlands and canyons.
PHOTO BY SOUTH DAKOTA TOURISM

FACING PAGE: Birch trees amid Black Hills spruce blaze with fall color along Spearfish Creek in the Black Hills National Forest.

ABOVE: Yellow sweet clover thrives on the rolling hills of Buffalo County.

FACING PAGE: Castle Rock rises grandly from the prairie in Butte County.

ABOVE: Canada geese in flight. These easily recognizable waterbirds fly south in autumn, passing migration routes generation to generation. PHOTO BY SOUTH DAKOTA TOURISM

FACING PAGE: Barely a ripple in sight, this glasslike pond in Marshall County reflects an equally calm sky.

ABOVE: A shy bison calf peeks through a tangle of wildflowers. PHOTO BY SOUTH DAKOTA TOURISM

RIGHT: The sun rises over a proud sandstone city in Badlands National Park.

ABOVE: A weathered barn sits at the base of the Black Hills in a valley near Custer.

FACING PAGE: This gravel road provides access to farmsteads in Davison County.

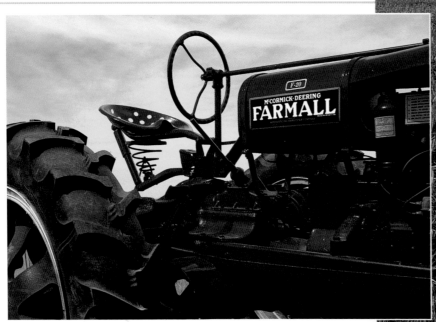

ABOVE: This 1939 Farmall F-20 is one of many antique tractors on display at the South Dakota Tractor Museum in Kimball.

RIGHT: Round straw bales dot this recently harvested field in Fall River County.

ABOVE: A lone bison under the big South Dakota sky in Wind Cave National Park.

FACING PAGE: Early morning sun reveals a palette of color in this shortgrass prairie, part of Wind Cave National Park.

ABOVE: Colorful striated badlands beneath a moody sky in Badlands National Park.

FACING PAGE: Right before a rainstorm in the Buffalo Gap National Grasslands.

ABOVE: A prairie pothole at Samuel H. Ordway, Jr. Memorial Preserve is a mirror for the full moon.

FACING PAGE: Prairie potholes collect and hold water from snowmelt and rain, forming valuable habitat for waterfowl and helping control flooding.

ABOVE: Morning light and shadow at Badlands National Park.

FACING PAGE: Ice holds captive the still waters of Stockade Lake in Custer State Park.

PRECEDING PAGES: Storm clouds gather over these classic Badlands National Park formations.

ABOVE: American Indian tradition is preserved and celebrated throughout the state. PHOTO BY SOUTH DAKOTA TOURISM

FACING PAGE: A display of native dancing at the Black Hills Powwow in Rapid City. PHOTO BY SOUTH DAKOTA TOURISM

ABOVE: Forget-me-nots ask for attention in the Black Hills National Forest.

RIGHT: A creek rushes through grasslands at Wind Cave National Park.

ABOVE: Spearfish Canyon was formed around 50 million years ago when fast-moving water eroded away the softer rock that used to fill this area.

FACING PAGE: A ray of sun shines across the top of this rocky cliff on the shore of Rock Creek in Palisades State Park.

ABOVE: Draft horses pull a wagon toward the one-room schoolhouse at the Laura Ingalls homestead in DeSmet.

FACING PAGE: Boundless prairie and sky on the Rosebud Reservation in the southern part of the state.

ABOVE: A small creek carves a path through this Marshall County prairie.

FACING PAGE: Oak Creek and the surrounding wetlands provide wildlife habitat on the Rosebud Reservation.

Time to bring in the cattle at the Krogman Ranch in Mellette County.

ABOVE: Yellow sweet clover brightens the broad hills of Gregory County.

FACING PAGE: Native plants prosper in this wetlands area in Sanborn County.

ABOVE: Brilliant fall foliage on display in Custer State Park.

RIGHT: An admixture of color: red rock cliffs, evergreen trees, and autumn-tinted ash trees in Custer State Park.

ABOVE: Father and son fish on a summer evening along the Missouri River near Pierre.

FACING PAGE: A spring sky reflected in wetlands on the Rosebud Reservation.

FOLLOWING PAGES: Granite badlands formations are reflected in perfectly still Sylvan Lake in Custer State Park.

ABOVE: A Jet Skier speeds across the surface of the Missouri River near Pierre.

FACING PAGE: It's a tight fit for this RV going through a tunnel in The Needles at Custer State Park.

The sun sets over Shadehill Lake, part of Shadehill Recreation Area.

ABOVE: Old wagon wheels at an antiques shop in Custer.

RIGHT: Rise and shine at Thill's Dairy Farm in Davison County.

The warm light of sunset gleams on ripples in the Missouri River.

Signs of the past abound at Samuel H. Ordway, Jr. Memorial Preserve: glacier-carved prairie potholes, granite boulders, tepee rings, and the remnants of early homesteads.

ABOVE: South Dakota State University's Miss Rodeo 2003, Marie Schaller, poses with her horse in Wessington Springs.

RIGHT: Strolling Deadwood's main street is like going back in time to the Wild West. Deadwood is where famous gunslinger Wild Bill Hickock was shot while playing poker.

ABOVE: The famous Old Longhorn Saloon in Scenic is decorated with ox skulls, sawdust floors, and tractor-seat stools.

FACING PAGE: These tepees were constructed as set pieces for the movie *Crazy Horse*. PHOTO BY SOUTH DAKOTA TOURISM

ABOVE: Inside Rushmore Cave. A one-hour guided tour takes visitors through the cavern's many rooms and narrow passageways.
PHOTO BY SOUTH DAKOTA TOURISM

FACING PAGE: Mammoth Site of Hot Springs, South Dakota, is the world's largest mammoth research facility. PHOTO BY SOUTH DAKOTA TOURISM

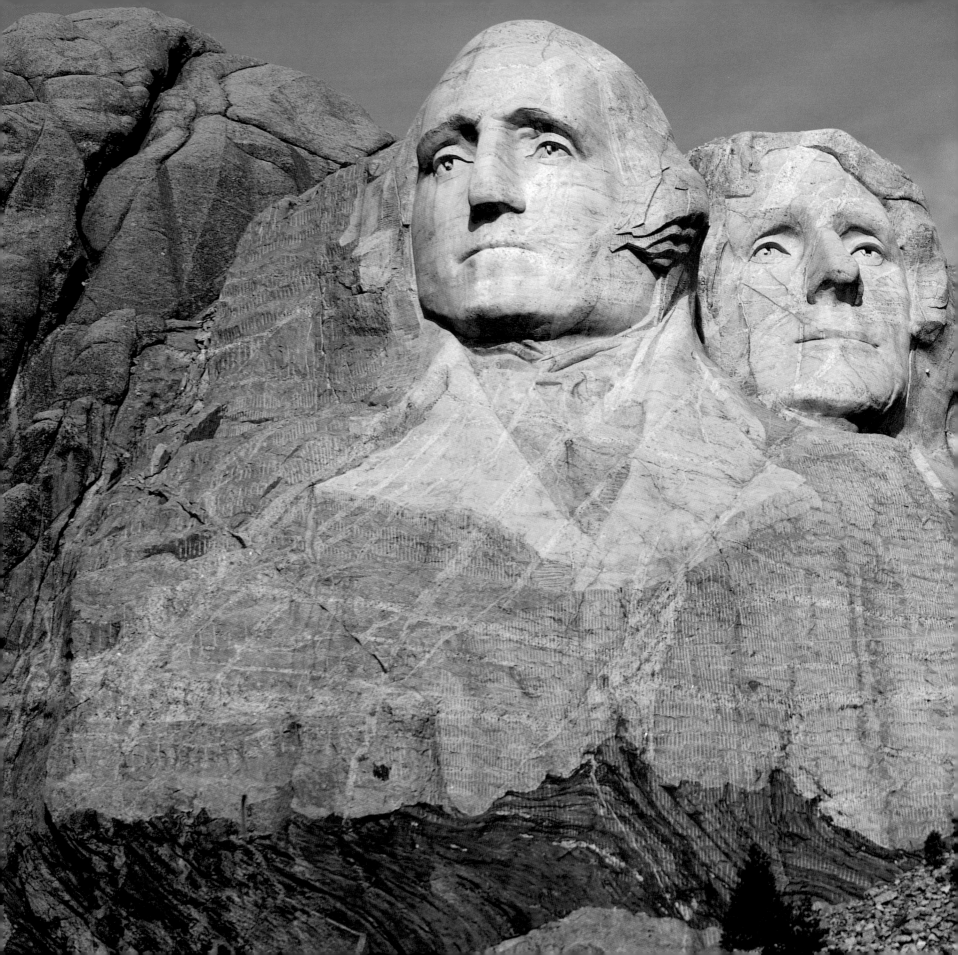

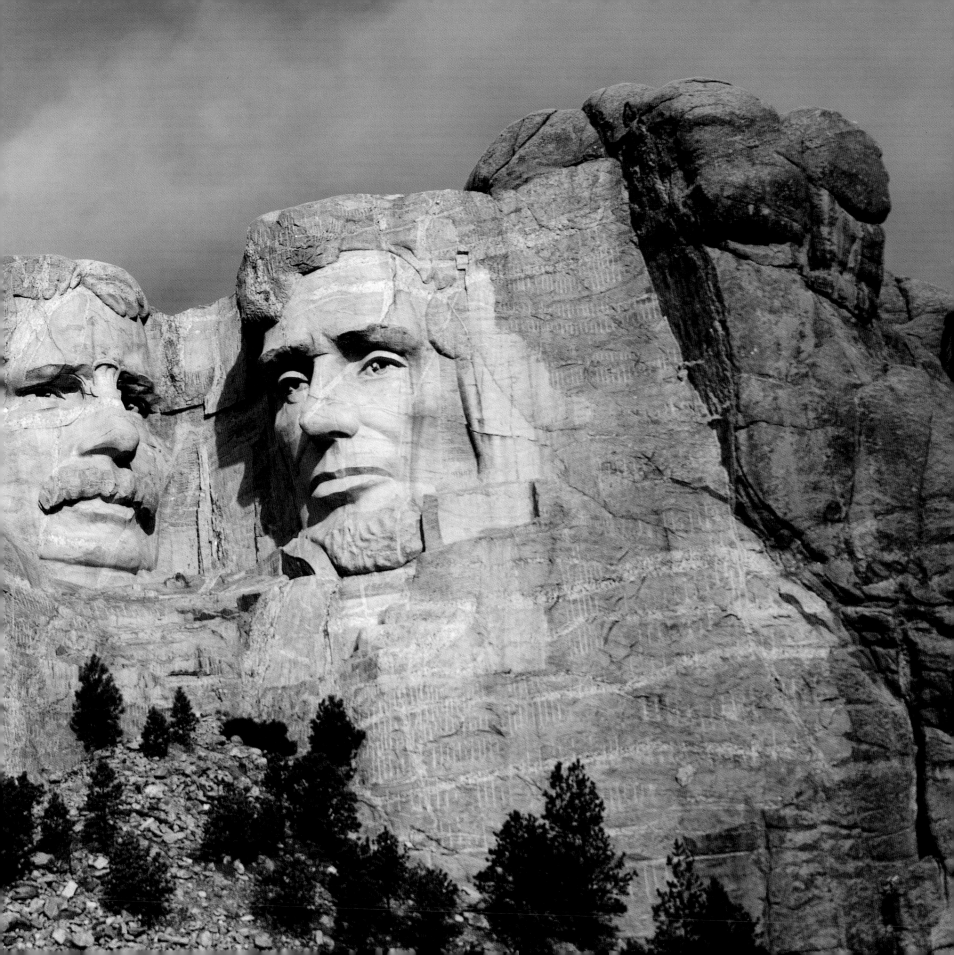

ABOVE: A prominent landmark on the edge of the prairie, Bear Butte is still a sacred place for many plains Indian tribes.

FACING PAGE: A wash as it appears after a rainstorm in Gregory County.

PRECEDING PAGES: Completed in 1941, Mt. Rushmore represents the first 150 years of American history, featuring 60-foot-tall busts of George Washington, Thomas Jefferson, Theodore Roosevelt, and Abraham Lincoln.

ABOVE: A lone cottonwood tree watches over this Gregory County prairie.

FACING PAGE: Prairie grasses and a wetlands pond in the quiet of mid-winter.

ABOVE: Stone barracks at Fort Sisseton, which was built in 1864 and is now preserved as a state park.

FACING PAGE: Fort Sisseton, in northwestern South Dakota, was restored by Works Progress Administration employees in the 1930s.

Agriculture remains an important South Dakota industry. The state's major crops include corn, wheat, and sunflower seeds.

Many of South Dakota's first citizens were homesteaders who'd heard about the fertile farmland in the eastern part of the state.

ABOVE: A radiant Rocky Mountain iris blooms in Custer State Park.

FACING PAGE: A closeup look at Ponderosa pine trunks and an understory of golden banner in the Black Hills National Forest.

ABOVE: Look closely to find the mule deer hiding in this badlands cave.
PHOTO BY SOUTH DAKOTA TOURISM

LEFT: The endless view from Pinnacles Overlook in Badlands National Park.

ABOVE: The ring-neck pheasant is South Dakota's state bird. PHOTO BY SOUTH DAKOTA TOURISM

FACING PAGE: The Grand River bisects the Grand River National Grasslands, near Lemmon.

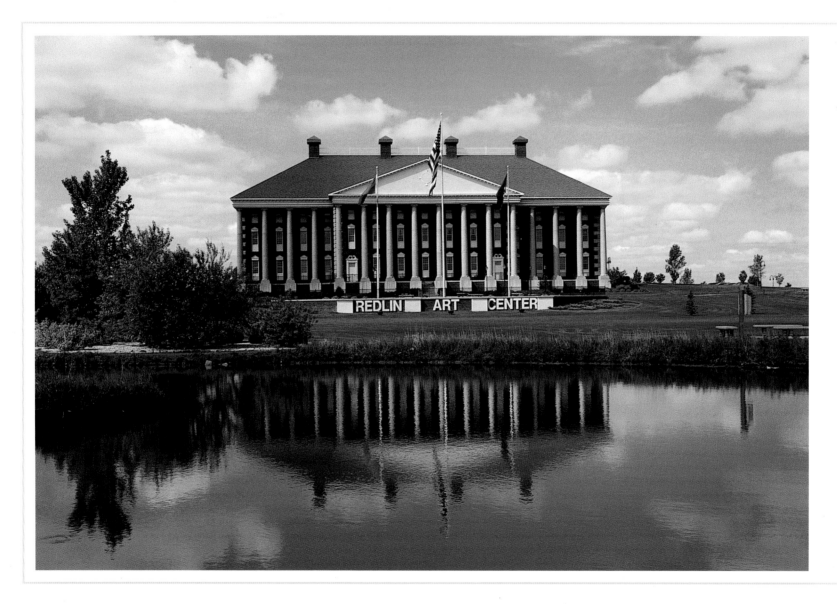

ABOVE: Redlin Art Center in Watertown features the oil paintings of Terry Redlin; the building was designed by his son, Charles.

FACING PAGE: South Dakota's Capitol, in Pierre, features handcrafted materials including carved woodwork, sculpted marble, cast brass, and hand-laid stone blocks.

Downtown Belle Fourche, pronounced "bell foosh" and translated as "beautiful fork."
The town is located at the confluence of the Redwater and Belle Fourche Rivers.

Vaun Boyd poses with his merchandise near the town of Custer.

ABOVE: Volunteers prepare to open the chute at the Wessington Springs Foothills Rodeo.

RIGHT: A cowgirl dismounts in a goat-tying event at Wessington Springs.

Huron is famous for its many spectacular outdoor murals; more are added each year.

The Alex Johnson Hotel in Rapid City was built in the 1920s and named for the vice president of the Chicago and Northwestern Railroad.

Interior view of the famous tourist destination Wall Drug.

ABOVE: A host of unique natural phenomena can be found in Sica Hollow State Park, including bogs that seep red liquid and tree stumps that seem to glow in the dark.

LEFT: Dramatic Sioux Falls is popular among visitors to Sioux Falls State Park.

ABOVE: Bendon Church in Kimball was built by Czech pioneers in 1893.

FACING PAGE: White loco blooms along Sage Creek in Badlands National Park.

Greeting a crisp winter day in Badlands National Park.

ABOVE: Vibrant dame's rockets shoot up from this riparian area in Lake Hiddenwood State Park.

FACING PAGE: Native to Eurasia, these purple dame's rockets grow next to a creek in Wind Cave National Park.

ABOVE: More than 62,000 American Indians live in South Dakota; most belong to the Sioux Nation.
PHOTO BY SOUTH DAKOTA TOURISM

LEFT: A herd of bison feeds and rests in this prairie within the boundaries of Custer State Park.

ABOVE: The world's largest pheasant roosts in Huron.

FACING PAGE: The exterior of the Mitchell Corn Palace is rebuilt
every year from thousands of bushels of corn, wheat, oats, and grasses.

ABOVE: Advertising for an antiques store in Henry.

FACING PAGE: A well-kept red barn reflected in a stock pond in Marshall County.

ABOVE: Mud cracks are a reminder of the harsh conditions found in Badlands National Park.

FACING PAGE: Millions of years of human history rest within the badlands of Badlands National Park. The park is home to the world's richest Oligocene Epoch fossil beds.

Little White River curves across the Rosebud Reservation.

The James River flows placidly through Sanborn County, providing myriad fishing and wildlife-viewing opportunities.

Winter snow cleverly hides from the setting sun in badlands fissures.

A scale model of the Crazy Horse Memorial with Crazy Horse Mountain, where work continues on the sculpture, in the background.

Grave of legendary Sioux leader Sitting Bull, on a hill near Mobridge.

ABOVE: Silvery Bridal Veil Falls drops gracefully into Spearfish Canyon, Black Hills National Forest.

FACING PAGE: Picturesque pond in Shadehill Recreation Area, nestled along the edge of the Shadehill Reservoir.

ABOVE: A rising full moon is framed by badlands formations.

FACING PAGE: Twin pinnacles reach for the sky in Badlands National Park.

ABOVE: A white-tailed deer forages in a South Dakota meadow.
PHOTO BY SOUTH DAKOTA TOURISM

LEFT: To get the best view of Roughlock Falls in Spearfish Canyon, visitors must wade into the creek—but the water is very cold!

ABOVE: The grasslands of western South Dakota provide habitat for the elusive prairie chicken. PHOTO BY SOUTH DAKOTA TOURISM

FACING PAGE: Young Ponderosa pines scatter throughout a field of yellow sweet clover in Wind Cave National Park.

ABOVE: Wind Cave Canyon is a popular bird-watching area within Wind Cave National Park.

FACING PAGE: Mountain goats graze in a valley below unmistakable Mt. Rushmore. PHOTO BY SOUTH DAKOTA TOURISM

ABOVE: Wild rose dripped with dew in Wind Cave National Park.

FACING PAGE: Fog creeps into Sage Creek Valley, part of Badlands National Park.

Real cowboys still ranch and ride the prairies and grasslands of South Dakota.